Redefining the Role of the Youth Worker

A Manifesto of Integration

APRIL L. DIAZ

FOREWORD BY DR. KARA POWELL

The contemporary church models we employ today emerged from the youth ministry models of the 1960s and 70s. Similarly, the future of the church is being shaped today by the new models of youth ministry being explored. Diaz takes us on a journey through her own church's changing understanding of student development and in the process provides more than a new model of youth ministry, but a new vision for the church itself.

Skye Jethani
Executive Editor, Leadership Journal

April Diaz in her brilliant book *Redefining the Role of the Youth Leader* insightfully deconstructs the sacred cows of youth ministry with humility and candid honesty. April is a voice to be listened to. She is one of the next generation of leaders that embodies the fearless heart of Jesus. Don't mess with her! Get this book now or miss out on some proven praxis from the front lines!

Dave Gibbons
Founder of Newsong Church and XEALOTS.ORG

April is one of the sharpest people I know, and it shows in this fantastic little book! In these pages she will encourage you, challenge you, motivate you and at times frustrate you... which is why you will be glad you read it. Thanks, April, for moving the youth ministry ball a little further down the field!

Kurt Johnston
Pastor to Students, Saddleback Church

April passionately reminds us of the heart of our work— relationships with and within the Body of Christ. Her steps toward redefining the role of the youth worker are echoed in the words of others who have also experienced similar "holy discontent" with status quo youth ministry. If you're hungry for more, see a link that might be missing, are frustrated in the way the church and youth ministry segregate...then you've found an exceptional place to begin: right here, with April.

Brooklyn Lindsey
Youth Pastor, Highland Park Church of the Nazarene,
Lakeland, FL

This book is a refreshing invitation to re-imagine both the depth and praxis of youth ministry and the Church. It's filled with many compelling reasons and inspiring stories of why one church chose to live differently for the sake of young people. Truly admirable and worth reading.

Charles Lee
CEO of Ideation & Author of Good Idea. Now What?

For years many of us have known that something wasn't quite right with how we've been ministering to students all these years. In *Redefining the Role of the Youth Worker,* April Diaz has taken us one step closer to providing us with a clear and compelling vision for a desperately needed new vision for youth ministry. April's extensive history and experience, keen mind, and love for kids, families and the church all combine to help the newcomer or most seasoned veteran take the leap into a more theological, long-term and practical world of our ministry to our young.

Chap Clark, Ph.D
Author, Hurt 2.0: Inside the World of Today's Teenagers
Professor of Youth, Family, and Culture, Fuller Seminary

I don't know one youth worker who isn't interested in finding ways to expand the spiritual formation framework in their faith community. Practical yet extremely thoughtful, this excellent book will help you think, be and do your way toward the possibility of a more holistic and full-bodied approach to developing true integrated faith communities of practice.

Chris Folmsbee
Church of the Resurrection, Leawood, KS

In *Redefining the Role of the Youth Worker*, April Diaz invites us on a journey of ministry reformation, as she translates the findings of the Sticky Faith research project into a model that actually works in the real-life trenches of youth ministry. There is little doubt that now is the time for bold experimentation around the dream of building student ministries that actually build life-long faith in the next generation, and April is one of the early cartographers of the future landscape of youth ministry.

Mark DeVries
Author of Family-Based Youth Ministry,
Founder of Ministry Architects

April is a youth ministry hero. She has a proven track record as an innovative leader and advocate/disciple-maker of kids and teens. In this book she shares her secrets and insights into developing an out-of-the-box leadership strategy that keeps kids grounded in faith over the long haul. This is a youth ministry must-read!

Dr. Steve Gerali
Globally recognized expert in
adolescence and youth ministry,
Author of the book series, What Do I Do When Teenagers...

I read this book immediately after wrestling with some Youth For Christ veterans about needed shifts in a ministry leader's job description and just prior to interviewing candidates for my church's open position in youth ministry. The timing was perfect, bringing sweet clarity to my own gnawing convictions. As a bonus, the book reads like a caffeinated conversation with your spunky, irrepressible and street-wise friend. April and Newsong Church are onto a really important course correction for God's people and I'm grateful that she's made the effort to share her insights with us all.

Dr. Dave Rahn
Senior Vice President, Chief Ministry Officer,
Youth for Christ/USA

April does an incredible job of helping you as a youth worker, church leadership team look at how to best serve the teens, their families and the whole of the church through this evaluation and discerning process. April helps you as a leader wrestle through how to manage change in your context. It is an excellent book that needs to be read by every youth worker who wants to continue to impact the lives of teens throughout their faith journey and not just a few years of their lives while in school. I would highly recommend this book to youth workers, church leadership teams and all of those wondering how do we impact the lives of our early adults.

Marti Burger
Director of Youth and Family Ministries,
Evangelical Covenant Church

April Diaz's strong vision, clear communication and challenging optimism for the local church bleed through each page. Hard won wisdom from many faithful years in the trenches of ministry have produced a true gift for church leaders and everyone who cares about the spiritual development of students. Please allow her vibrant words to capture your heart and influence your efforts—do not delay!

Mindy Caliguire
Founder and President of Soul Care;
Executive Director of Engage International
Author of Soul Care Resources series

I'm a huge fan of April and her view of youth ministry. This book pushes me and will push you to change the way you think about how a church should care for its young people. April makes a strong case that we need to change and gives good examples of how their church changed. It wasn't always easy but in the end they got the results they were hoping for.

Dr. Lars K. Rood
Associate Pastor of Family Life,
Bellevue Presbyterian Church

Redefining the Role of the Youth Worker
A Manifesto of Integration

Copyright © 2013 by April L. Diaz

Publisher: Mark Oestreicher
Managing Editor: Anne Marie Miller
Editor: Laura Gross
Design: Adam McLane
Author Headshot: Hanju Lee
Creative Director: Daniel Webster

Scripture quotations marked NLT are taken from the Holy Bible,
New Living Translation, Copyright © 1996, 2004, 2007. Used
by permission of Tyndale House Publishers, Inc., Carol Stream,
Illinois 60188. All rights reserved.

Scripture quotations marked NIV are taken from THE HOLY
BIBLE, New International Version®, NIV® Copyright © 1973,
1978, 1984, 2011 by Biblica, Inc.™ Used by permission. All rights
reserved worldwide.

ISBN-13: 978-0-9887413-7-9
ISBN-10: 0988741377

The Youth Cartel, LLC
www.theyouthcartel.com
Email: info@theyouthcartel.com
Born in San Diego | Printed in the U.S.A.

Contents

A Note from the Publisher

I've known April Diaz as a youth ministry friend for a number of years (we were both Junior High Pastors, and it's a pretty small tribe). So we often talked—at great length—about youth ministry ideas and theory and problems. And it didn't seem out of the blue when she called me one day, a few years ago now, to ask for my input on rethinking the position of Youth Pastor at her church. She had an opportunity (which she describes in this book) to consider some serious reinvention.

We talked a bunch and exchanged a dozen emails. Eventually, April sent me a draft of a job description unlike any youth worker role I'd ever seen, one that gave me hope and made me nervous at the same time. We bantered about possible titles (because April, rightly so, felt that language was extremely important in communicating that this isn't just the same ol' same ol').

And I watched from afar as she made her courageous hire.

It was all pretty amazing, to be honest. We asked her to speak at The Summit, an event hosted by The Youth

Cartel that has the flavor of a TED event – provocative ideas and creative thinking all geared to spark your imagination. I asked April to speak for 15 minutes on a very focused topic, based on her story over the past year. I asked her to present on the topic of "Redefining the Role of the Youth Worker." (If that title sounds familiar, uh, that's because it's the name of the title of the book you're reading.)

April nailed it. It was one of the best talks at The Summit. Later that same day, I asked her to write this book. I asked her to imagine it as a very short book, a feisty (but humble) little manifesto, a hopeful narrative about change and integration and the possibility of a new way and a new day.

This isn't a "throw the baby out with the bathwater" book. I have very little tolerance for people who suggest that youth ministry isn't biblical and should therefore be completely shut down. But we *simply must stop the systematic isolation of teenagers in our churches*. Please.

So, explore with me. We have a lovely and brave and fun and honest guide in April Diaz.

Mark Oestreicher
Publisher | The Youth Cartel

Foreword
by Dr. Kara Powell

When you meet April Diaz, you won't soon forget her.

At least that was my experience when she and I first met for lunch five years ago. A few mutual friends had suggested we connect since we live about an hour from each other, and April graciously drove to Pasadena.

I have two vivid memories from that lunch.

Okay, actually three. The blue corn tostada salad I ordered was delicious.

I also recall that I shared far more with April than I ever expected to tell someone that I was meeting for the first time. Talking with April about what God was showing me in that season and the new insights I was gaining about God's grace was like my own "theological therapy" session.

In addition, I remember that eight days after our lunch, I received a package from April—a bottle of lotion called "Grace." I was touched that not only had April sent me the lotion, but its title mirrored the life labs

God was using to teach me more about His amazing, saving gift.

My lunch with April reflects what you will learn about her in this book—she is a fantastic listener, a creative follower of Christ, and she cares deeply about God and people and connecting the two.

By reading this book, you won't just learn *about* April. You'll learn *from* her. When we at the Fuller Youth Institute launched our Advisory Council (a group of national advisors to help us determine our direction and initiatives), we were thrilled when April agreed to join that team. We've watched April lead others and practice the very 360-degree leadership that she champions in this book within her congregation. We've cheered on April and her team as they've made some needed but challenging course corrections to redefine their youth ministry as well as their church's discipleship across the generations. Perhaps my favorite part of this book is that it gives you and your team an insider look at the change process.

As much as I liked that "Grace" lotion, I love this book even more.

Shout-Outs

Writing a book is no joke. For months I didn't even tell anyone I had agreed to write my first book. My FIRST book! I love a challenge, but this was intimidating. Just like any good story, I didn't write this in my own brilliance. Not even close.

First, a million thanks to Marko and The Youth Cartel. You've believed in me for years and beyond what I could see in myself. Thank you for asking the tough questions, pushing me toward deep change, providing raucous affirmation, and making me laugh. I'm honored that you wanted to publish this work. I also believe editors are the unsung heroes of any published work. Wild thanks to Laura Gross and Anne Marie Miller for your expertise, patience, and graciousness with this first-time author.

Heartfelt gratitude to those who've informed my leadership the most along the way: Brad Johnson, Dan Webster, Bo Boshers, Jeanne Stevens, Dr. Steve Gerali, Rebecca and Josh Lujan Loveless, Dr. Kara Powell, Dave Gibbons, Dr. Scott Cormode, Hendre D Coetzee, and my friends from the Middle School Pastors' Summit. You've caused me to love, learn, and serve to the best of my ability.

Perhaps the greatest development of the ideas in this book came about from my cohort experience with the Fuller Youth Institute. Kara, Brad, Irene, and the entire FYI team took us on a transformational journey that's produced lasting change in our context. Thank you for the incredible investment you've made into our community and so many others. You are pioneers in this movement!

What began as an idea turned into a possibility and then a reality for our church. I'm so grateful that my church, Newsong, didn't hold method sacred but trusted us to explore and innovate. Thank you for letting us risk for the sake of our students' future. Special thanks to Daniel Roach, Newsong Church staff, and the students, parents, and volunteer leaders of Evolve and Fusion (Newsong's middle school and high school ministries) for going on this journey with me. Mike Park, you are the answer to a prayer, and a dream fulfilled for our community (Joshua 1). We're blessed to have you lead us into the future.

Immeasurable thanks to my parents, brothers, and extended family, as well as to my Human Development team at Newsong, and my intercessory prayer team. You all were reckless enthusiasts of my writing, committed to praying, and hopelessly supportive from the beginning. And thanks to our Village—you know who you are.

Clearly, anything of eternal value in these pages is the result of a gracious and loving God. How I was able to write this book while working a full-time job and raising three kids under the age of five is proof God exists! All the glory is his, and anything of value is the favor of the Holy Spirit for his children.

Finally, thank you to the best partner a girl could ask for. Brian, our life is borderline insane but filled with adventure, wonder, and care. Thank you for walking with me through the highs and lows of our life together. I love you beyond words.

Judah Abebayehu, Addise Aster Tarike, and Asher Zacarias, this book is for you. It is your momma's deepest prayer and most urgent desire that you would grow up to madly love Jesus and his church. The ways we do youth ministry now and into the future are so you can learn to walk closely with your Creator. Your daddy and I love you . . . no matter what!

April L. Diaz
Irvine, California

Introduction

This is not a book about youth ministry. Well, it's not *entirely* about youth ministry. This is a book about the church and her relationship with teenagers. It's not a book about the organization but about the people of God. These pages offer an invitation for anyone who loves teenagers. This is a story, a calling, a vision for the church to be more whole, more cohesive, and longer lasting than the six or seven years that make up most youth ministries. In part, this book is a case study about one church who became captivated by a bigger vision for their teenagers and decided things needed to be different. Quite different. And it's a stake in the ground that things must be different in our churches and cities for the sake of this generation and the ones to come.

I'm greatly encouraged by how this conversation is gaining traction in the youth ministry world. God is awakening faith leaders to pay attention to the state of youth and their future in different ways. Questions are being asked. Changes are being implemented. Seismic shifts are happening. History is being made.

After nearly 15 years of youth ministry, I simply got tired of getting the same old results from my blood, sweat, and tears. I was tired of seeing the teenagers I'd loved and poured into over the years walk away from Christ and his church after leaving the safety and comfort of their homes and our ministry. For several decades, the church's approach to youth has more or less looked the same; but student culture, educational systems, and families have changed significantly.

This book doesn't have "THE answer" for your context, but it certainly has one suggestion that's been working for our local church. However, our answer came after a lengthy process. It was God's word to us "*for such a time as this*" (Esther 4:14). My prayer, though, is that this little book will provide a road map of sorts as your community does the hard work of discerning God's word to you and your people. Together, I believe this can be a new generation with dramatically different results for the sake of the kingdom and God's people.

It's time to take another look at our deepest dreams and discern what must change in order for us to realize those dreams. It's time to dream anew . . .

Chapter One

Why Reimagine?

> *But Jesus said, "Let the children come to me.*
> *Don't stop them!*
> *For the Kingdom of Heaven belongs to those who*
> *are like these children."*
> — Matthew 19:14 (NLT)

> *You can imagine fighting against 70 years of*
> *church culture has been a bit tough. As profes-*
> *sional youth workers, we have done such a great*
> *job over the years; it's hard for anyone to imagine*
> *why we would want to change.*
> — Alan Mercer, Executive Pastor
> Leawood Campus of Christ Community Church
> Kansas City, MO

I was raised in the church. Generations of my family have been committed followers of Jesus Christ. When I was five years old, I became a Christian at the Christian elementary school I attended. My best friend April (no, she wasn't imaginary) stood next to me as we asked Jesus into our hearts. In seventh grade, I rededicated my life to Jesus at summer camp when I understood that being a Christian wasn't just about heaven, it was about having a relationship with Jesus during this lifetime, too.

My parents are two of the most faithful, passionate, and generous disciples I know. They have poured their faith into my life, and it's been the best gift they could've given me. I've wrestled deeply with God in my own faith journey, but I never went through "rebellious" years or abandoned my faith altogether.

At 16 years old, I felt called into youth ministry. It wasn't the audible voice of God, but it was the next closest thing. I knew ministry with high school students was the place where I knew I'd pour my life. So I applied to Bible college (and was rejected!), and then I went on to intern in a church's high school ministry two months after my own high school graduation. After my calling was confirmed, I enrolled in a different Bible college and received my bachelor's degree in youth ministry and adolescent studies. For the majority of my adult life, I have been about the lives of middle school and high school students.

Now, I'm a mom. My sons are five and one; my daughter is three. Every night I pray aloud over my kids that they would "ask Jesus into their hearts very, very soon." More than anything else in the world, my husband and I desire for our three kids to know Christ and him crucified. We hope beyond all hope that they not only ask Jesus into their hearts, but also become madly in love with God and serve as world-changers in his kingdom. We pray they come to know the gospel as good news not because of anything they can do, but because of everything Jesus has done.

In our family we echo the belief of the Israelites' way of life shown in Deuteronomy 6, repeating God's commands *"again and again to your children. Talk about them when you are at home and when you are on the road, when you are going to bed and when you are getting up"* (verse 7). We desperately rely on our Village—friends and family—to help us in this mighty calling, because we are painfully aware of our inadequacies and limitations. Most of all, we pray. We pray our kids will experience a Romans 8 kind of love that will tether them to their Creator.

I am acutely aware that my story of lifelong discipleship is not the story of many. So what about them? What about the teenager who isn't born into a Christian family and brought to church every week? What about the adolescent who is lulled into a life of drugs, violence, or preoccupation with success? Or what about the student who doubts and questions everything about his or her faith but isn't met with acceptance? What about those 12-, 15-, and 18-year-olds? What happens to them?

Youth ministry hasn't always existed as we know it today. In fact, *youth ministry* is a term and a programmatic structure that's been around since the 1940s when parachurch youth ministries such as Young Life and Youth for Christ started popping up in the United States. And what we know of as church-based youth ministry first launched during the 1970s. But before churches created youth departments and hired youth pastors, teenagers were integrated into the life of the broader church. They didn't have their own Sunday services, middle school lock-ins, high school paintball events, and Bible studies written just for them. For better or worse, they were just a part of the larger life of the church. But that all began to change with the rise of parachurch ministries, and the American church has never been the same.

There has been so much good that's come from the rise of youth ministry programs and professionalized youth ministry. (I wouldn't have my college diploma or my first couple of jobs if youth ministry didn't become so valued in the church!) A couple of generations ago, millions of teenagers were reached through innovative and revolutionary organizations and churches, and that's how "youth ministry" was born. The focus, intentionality, and developmental specificity of reaching adolescents for the sake of Jesus and his kingdom was unprecedented and soon skyrocketed in effectiveness.

But over the past couple of decades, our culture has dramatically changed, and youth ministry has been slow to respond and find fresh ways to disciple the younger generation. Some of the most popular youth ministry and youth culture writings of the past decade have been raising the flag that there's a crisis of faith within the younger generation. Go to any youth ministry conference and you'll find seminars about how youth ministry is broken.

One definition of insanity is doing the same thing over and over again and expecting different results. When statistics and common sense reveal that 50+ percent of high school graduates leave the church and shelve their faith during college and beyond, something isn't working. What's even more sobering is "only 20 percent of college students who leave the church planned to do so during high school. The remaining 80 percent intended to stick with their faith—but didn't" (Powell and Griffin 2011, 15).

Tim Clydesdale, researcher and sociologist, identified this phenomenon as "lockbox faith." Imagine you're a high school student who's graduated and is now headed into your first year at the local community college or university. Now picture me handing you a giant Bible. You know the kind I mean—the ones with the extra-large print that only grandmas carry with them to church? That Bible represents your faith in Jesus Christ. "Lockbox faith" is a visual metaphor of what happens when students enter college (or wherever life takes them after high school). They take their giant grandma-style Bibles and put them into lockboxes for safekeeping. Then for the next several life-altering years of their lives, their faith is locked away. The silver lining to this phenomenon is that when college-age students put their faith in a lockbox, they are not discarding their faith altogether. They are keeping it safely locked up for later. (*Sticky Faith* further describes lockbox faith.)

The fact that you're reading this book is proof that you love adolescents too much and work way too hard to allow 50+ percent of them to walk away from life with Jesus. It's not enough to know that some of them will eventually wander back into faith after they've experienced the consequences of their lockbox faith years. For those of us who've worked with 20- and 30-somethings (this includes many of our youth ministry volunteers), we know the deep wounds, scars, and lifelong consequences that come from shelving one's faith for those all-important college years. Clydesdale's research raises a red flag on our intentionality toward preserving teenagers' faith after high school: "Given the seeming importance of retaining youth for most religious groups in the United States, it is striking how haphazardly most congregations go about it" (Clydesdale 2007, 205).

Yet as I look back over my years in youth ministry—pouring my life into the lives of teenagers—I must confess that my "results" reflect that 50 percent statistic. I confess that I've been quite haphazard about nurturing vibrant, lifelong faith in Jesus Christ. But people aren't mere statistics. These statistics are people I love: Andrea, Sydney, Vincent, Cassidy, Ian, Jessica, Daniel, Karis, Mychel, Alex. Their lives and stories are the compelling reasons why things need to change in my church and in yours, in my family and in yours.

Dare I say that maybe we're a little "insane" in our churches when we merely tweak youth ministry programming, series titles, and how we calendar events, and just hope that 50+ percent statistic will drop? I actually think our insanity is inextricably linked to our belief in lies: *It's not really that bad; things are getting better; this is only a phase.* We believe the lies that this is all it can be, and we continue the cycle of doing the same things year after year, all while expecting different results.

> *What we considered to be a standard approach to planning an entertainment-based youth ministry has brought eye-opening results to the lives of teenagers beyond high school. We've begun to asking the hard questions of how we go about youth ministry in a context that is still looking for entertainment-based options.*
> — Keegan Lenker

Something isn't working. Something desperately needs to change. When there's a systemic problem, a systemic change is required.

My proposition is that change starts with leadership. In the ever-changing face of student culture and the church, it's insane to believe we can go on doing business as usual. Changing our vision for the youth worker's role is fundamental to changing that statistic.

May I begin this book with a confession? In my church context, we were fairly content with being insane. We knew we weren't operating at full capacity, but students were still showing up. It's not like we'd totally destructed. We were tweaking things here and there, yet we still weren't seeing tangible results. I felt a holy discontent that things were not as they should be, and that discontent would not let me go. The catalyst for us in reimagining the role of the youth worker was a staffing transition that presented an opportunity for real change. But honestly, the catalyst should have been the names and stories of graduated teenagers who were deeply struggling in their faith or no longer walking with Jesus.

In each of the first three Gospels where Jesus discusses fasting, he speaks some haunting words, *"And no one puts new wine into old wineskins. For the old skins would burst from the pressure, spilling the wine and ruining the skins. New wine is stored in new wineskins so that both are preserved"* (Matthew 9:17; Mark 2:22; Luke 5:37-38, NLT). I wonder why Jesus declares these words in a discussion on fasting? What do fasting, prayer, and wine have to do with each other? My hunch is that Jesus was hinting at the ancient truth that with any necessary change and maturing growth, a period of fasting and reflection must come. (...and wine never hurts!)

What we are considering requires more than fancy programmatic tweaks or human ingenuity. We require something new, given to us by the Divine Creator. To be given new wine and a new wineskin is beyond us, beyond our human knowledge or finite experience.

Jesus hints that this need to fast—a need to create space in which to evaluate the old—contains deep, yet difficult wisdom that will transform our very souls and then impact our leadership and the teenagers we love.

May we begin our reimagining with the humility to confess we've messed up a few things along the way—despite our good intentions—and we are in need of the Great Sommelier to make some new wine for us to drink from a new vessel.

Questions to Consider

- Are you convinced things need to change in youth ministry? If not, is the current reality more dangerous than pursuing the unknown?

- What do you think the following groups' perspectives and expectations of youth ministry are?

  - Students

  - Parents

  - Church leadership

  - Congregation

  - Graduates

- As you think about your last few graduating classes, how many are still involved in a local church?

  - What percentage of them has a relationship with Jesus Christ?

  - How many of them have an active faith in Jesus Chris?

  - Where do you see insanity at work and a need for change in your context?

- How might God be inviting you to fast so you are able to receive something new?

Chapter Two

Evaluating the Old

> *"Forget the former things;*
> *do not dwell on the past.*
> *See, I am doing a new thing!*
> *Now it springs up; do you not perceive it?*
> *I am making a way in the wilderness*
> *and streams in the wasteland."*
> — Isaiah 43:18-19 (NIV)

> *It's not new; we've just gotten away from it.*
> — Lars Rood, Pastor, Family Life Ministries
> Bellevue Presbyterian, Bellevue, WA

If you have a conversation with a veteran youth worker, I'm certain you'll hear at least hints of unhappiness at the estimated "50 percent of teenagers walk away from their faith and the church after high school" statistic. Other youth workers' reactions will range anywhere from frustration with the church or with parents to a full-on a rant about all that's broken within American youth ministry. I've yet to meet an experienced youth worker who's satisfied with the current reality. And rarely will I hear the statistics refuted. There's just too much to refute; plus, our anecdotal evidence matches the research.

Inevitably, when we risk exposing what we've been doing and the results from that activity, it will require unbridled honesty, courage, humility, and security in our identity in Christ. It's such a risky act; I actually don't know that we'll go there unless we're faced with a demanding reason. It's unnatural for us to fix what's broken unless we must—we hit bottom, we are exposed, we are captivated by a vision greater than the reality in which we are currently living. But more and more churches and faith leaders are hitting a metaphorical bottom. They are tired of doing the same things and expecting different results.

My Church's Journey

In my local church context, our journey actually started in 2008 as we began following the College Transition Project led by the Fuller Youth Institute (FYI)[1]. We were growing tired of graduating full classes of committed Christians, only to watch them drift away from Jesus and his church during their college years. So we examined FYI's findings and compared them to our own reality, asked questions, created new language

---

[1]Check out StickyFaith.org for more information.

within our leadership and youth ministry, and redefined what "success" looks like.

Then in 2010, our church went through staff reorganization. Values such as equipping volunteer lead ministries and streamlining ministries to become more collaborative and intergenerational became the priority over hiring more professional staff. As a member of the executive leadership team, I was able to speak into these fundamental shifts for our future, and encourage us to forge a new way forward.

The true impetus for redefining the role of the youth worker was a catalytic staffing transition in 2011. It presented us with an opportunity for real change and allowed us to dream anew. When our youth pastor accepted a different position within our church, our first step was to seek wise counsel. Very quickly it became clear that we needed to develop a lengthy assessment. This systematic yet creative process led us down a road and presented ideas that I never would have imagined if I'd simply tweaked our youth pastor job description and begun the search to fill that vacant position.

Let me pause for a minute to make a disclaimer: the youth pastor who chose to leave his position was amazing. Daniel was truly one of the best youth pastors in the country. He was a skilled leader with strong character and a deep love for teenagers and their families. He was also a gifted teacher with great capacity for capturing the attention of an audience. He was excellent at building teams of people to invest into the lives of our teenagers. The way he developed people and programs with limited resources was beyond commendable. In fact, he was totally on board when we began discussing how to redefine the role of the youth worker. He worked tirelessly with our team to ensure that we moved in this direction. So if you find yourself or your church in a role like Daniel's, know there is nothing but love for who you are and what you do. Know that it was someone similar to you who raised a flag and wanted something more. It was with Daniel's blessing and evaluation that the dream was made possible.

Now back to our process. At the request of our lead pastor, our team began a thorough, month-long assessment. The first level was to identify the defining and dominant characteristics of our surrounding youth culture. On a half page, we named three current overarching characteristics of national youth culture and the specific ways they played out in our local context:

1. We live in a coffeehouse culture. More "attractive" youth ministry doesn't work like it used to.

- Bigger isn't better. Relational closeness and depth is far more effective (even if it's fabricated intimacy from social media connections).
- Relational boldness and challenging our students' faith are priorities.

2. Family systems value education and college resume building more than church involvement.
   - The church doesn't dictate involvement. Students select what they will achieve and what will better their future success.
   - "If you build it, they will come" doesn't work unless it adds explicit values to their lives.
   - If the church can respond to the culture through service hours and leadership development, this will add value to the students' resume building. This will speak to the real and felt needs of students.

3. Focus activities or eliminate programming because students are too busy to gather more than once per week.
   - Asking students to meet as a youth group during the week is complicated.
   - Retreats are mini-monastic experiences for students.
   - Local and global experiences are priceless.

- Nationally, high school youth ministry involvement diminishes.

(Note: This assessment was done in May 2011. Since then, these characteristics are already a bit different. However, this was an important step in our process.)

Next, we diagnosed the middle school and high school ministries' current reality in light of our vision statement, which wasn't going to change: "Holistic transformation for the journey of a lifetime." In fact, our original vision compelled us to reimagine the role of the youth worker and the ways we expressed ministry with teenagers. In the current reality overview, we appraised the general highs and lows of each ministry's status, then dug a little deeper into the status of volunteers, weekly programs, leadership development, and special events. The overall assessment was especially challenging and freeing, as we gave ourselves permission to call out the best and worst of our ministry.

After completing this big-picture overview, we essentially took a snapshot of the last five years of youth ministry in our church. In quantitative terms, we then listed the staffing realities and transitions, as well as the attendance trends at our weekly gatherings and annual retreats. Following the quantitative review, we evaluated the annual programs and events of our ministry. We meticulously reviewed the annual calendar and named each event, how many times per year we did it, what the desired purpose and outcome was, and the amount of time required. After each event evaluation, we noted a recommendation of whether or not to continue based on past effectiveness. However, at this point in the process, we did not make a recommendation based on future vision. We also made note of those events we'd done during the past five years but had now stopped doing, including a brief rationale as to why.

At that point in our evaluation, we paused. We pored over the qualitative and quantitative data we'd collected, and we began to pray. We prayed God would illuminate a way forward for our church. We asked God to bubble to the surface any activity or event that was important to the kingdom and the future of the church. We grieved over those times when our work had been done apart from the leading of the Holy Spirit. We repented for not keeping in step with the Spirit (Galatians 5:25) and not doing only what we saw the Father doing (John 5:19). We worshipped and praised God for those times when we saw God doing what only God can do. We laughed as we recalled some really great memories of doing life together.

Then, we waited.

Over the next months, God began clarifying our future. We captured high-level ideas about our values and structure. We named philosophical shifts we needed to make and claimed God's desired place for us in the kingdom. We proposed to our lead pastor the practical future for our middle school and high school ministries, and we redefined the role of the youth worker.

Practically, we said we wanted to move forward in alignment with our church's vision. We knew that if our youth ministry's vision didn't align with our church's vision, we'd be fighting a losing battle. We articulated our goal as *missional life together*, while creating age-appropriate experiences that would prepare teenagers for the next season of their lives and engagement with the whole church community.

In order to accomplish that goal, we said we needed to focus on:

- Thinking about initiatives, not programs
- Finding meaningful places for adolescent involvement in the overall church
- Creating specialized experiences for community and learning, which meant thinking about formation-forward, theologically sound, and

developmentally specific experiences for teenagers

- Altering the 5:1 ratio, with five adults investing in every teenager, not just one adult ministering to five teenagers—It's not about finding five small-group leaders for every teenager, but five adults who love every teenager and are committed to their lifelong faith. These five adults could be relatives, educators, family friends, or church people. This is a key idea for nurturing long-term faith trumpeted by Chap Clark and found in Fuller Youth Institute's Sticky Faith research.

- Hosting two retreats per year—I've always said that attending one weekend retreat is like experiencing a whole year in a weekly small group. The foci of these retreats would be communal and experiential in nature, and they would hyperfocus on an area to catalyze spiritual formation.

- Hosting three mission experiences per year—Ideally, this would look like three to four days locally, one global experience, and one local experience exclusively for eighth through tenth graders.

- Customizing the development of our juniors and seniors to more intentionally prepare them for life after high school - If the research is correct, six out of seven graduating high school students don't feel prepared for life after high school.

- Integrating Jesus into everyday life—All of our training and equipping would be focused on connecting with Jesus'presence in every circumstance. (See Skye Jethani's book *With: Reimagining the Way You Relate to God* for an excellent theology of how we've messed up our understanding and relationship with Jesus.)

- Sharing stories of a future hope where all of the above is already happening within our ministry

Our Common Journey

One of the most valuable steps in our journey was participating in Fuller Youth Institute's Sticky Faith Cohort (2010). When a group of youth workers from past cohorts were asked about evaluating the old and pursuing a new thing, they responded with several firsthand accounts about evaluating their ministry. Many of their comments fell into two dominant categories.

First, a major obstacle several churches experienced was overcoming the mental models and expectations from parents and the overall church. Perhaps you've experienced something similar. It's the idea that youth ministry is a separate "program" of the church, rather than a part of the whole body of Christ. The second prevailing reflection was that parents in particular had a strong bias that the youth ministry—not the parents—would be the conduit by which lasting faith would be developed in their kids' lives.

As I've talked with youth workers from all over the country, and from a variety of denominations and church backgrounds, these are maybe two of the most dominant, common obstacles we identify as we assess our current reality. Though youth ministry has been around for only a couple of generations, the inherent beliefs about the roles of the family, the church, and the youth ministry have been deeply ingrained in how we think faith is grown and sustained in our teenagers. (See *Think Orange: Imagine the Impact When Church and Family Collide* by Reggie Joiner for practical ideas on how to equip parents.)

Your Unique Journey

I'm a huge fan of not reinventing the wheel (a.k.a. stealing others' best work) and of contextualizing everything to custom-fit our local community. As you evaluate your ministry, I'm not entirely sure what your journey will look like. But if you asked me for help, we'd probably meet up at my favorite local coffeeshop.

We'd sit outside on a cloudless, 70-something–degree day in SoCal, and I would likely frame our conversation with these three questions:

1. *What's causing the holy discontent within your spirit?* There's a reason you're feeling some dissonance, frustration, and desire for something else. Take that question and those emotions before the Lord and see what he has to say about that holy discontent. You may be surprised what he reveals. One thing I know is that change is often initiated by someone who's been given the spiritual gift of leadership. That gift has been gracefully given to you to inspire change and influence people toward a preferred future. Steward that gift well.

2. *Who else is "with you" in this discontent?* Beginning to identify a team of people who could assess and

> *Curious as it may be, few things keep churches more stuck than their successes. Here's the irony: Sustainable youth ministries fail all the time; they thrive in a culture of experimentation, innovation and creativity. It is floundering youth ministries that often remain paralyzed, unable to risk, stuck in a nostalgic obsession with past success.*
> — Mark DeVries, Sustainable Youth Ministry

lead with you is important. You need someone(s) who you can "talk out loud" with you as you brainstorm questions and possible solutions. You'll need a cheerleader or two who will fight for you when you get discouraged and feel defeated.

As you and I are sitting together and drinking iced green tea or a non-fat latte, I'd strongly encourage you not to move forward in this brave endeavor until you've established an intercessor team to cover you, your family, and your ministry in prayer. As you begin to push back on ground that the enemy has (temporarily) taken, you'll experience spiritual warfare and attacks. The enemy hates what we are looking to do. So to think that you can get away without having a strong backing of prayer is just foolish and proud.

I was foolish and proud in this area for almost the first 15 years of my pastoral work. I occasionally asked people to pray with me and for me, but it was far from active and intentional. I didn't have any idea about the powers that are at work around my family and me as a result of the spiritual work I do. In the past couple of years, I've instituted a prayer shield of 15+ people who have a gift of intercessory prayer and are committed to pray for my ministry and my family. I send them updates and requests; but predominantly they listen to God and pray according to the promptings of the Holy

Spirit. I can honestly say my ministry is different as a result of these faithful warriors and teammates. (Note: If you'd like more specific instruction on how to form a prayer shield, please feel free to contact me directly.)

3. *Does our church's process of evaluating the old help you? Or do you need to evaluate it in another way?* I'm sharing our process in order to help you jump-start your process as much as possible. We applied the wisdom and counsel of several sharp spiritual leaders to craft ours. So if it can serve you in any way, please use it. However, you know your context better than I do; areas that we didn't evaluate may be a must for you, while other areas may prove unimportant.

Questions to Consider

- What's holding you back from going through a systematic, creative assessment process? Is that reason enough not to do the assessment?

- If you could snap your fingers and change one thing about your role with teenagers and/or your church, what would it be?

- If we had coffee together, how would you respond to those three questions?

- Who are 5 to 10 intercessors you could enlist as the beginnings of your prayer shield?

Chapter Three

Redefining the Role

> *Direct your children onto the right path,*
> *and when they are older, they will not leave it.*
> — Proverbs 22:6 (NLT)

> *I am now leading the team from early childhood*
> *through 55+ in creating an environment of col-*
> *laboration.*
> — Keegan Lenker, Pastor of Intergenerational
> Discipleship, First Church of the Nazarene,
> Pasadena, CA

Our journey has been a long one—haphazard at times, wandering but never lost, ever seeking how and what this would look like for our community. When we moved from reimagining to redefining the role of the youth worker and youth ministry at our church, we made a dogmatic statement: We were NOT hiring a youth pastor. A "youth pastor" job title came with very clear expectations of what this person would and would not do. We needed to re-envision our community toward what this person would be responsible for, as well as the church's vision regarding the youth. *Who* we hired would be just as important as *what* we held him or her accountable to do (and not do!).

I grew up in a small, über-conservative church. During college, I volunteered at a small charismatic church and a mid-sized Baptist church. My pastoral work has led me to two megachurches in two different parts of the country. I've spoken, consulted, and become friends with leaders from a broad spectrum of economic, social, ethnic, and theological perspectives. Now, when I look across the landscape of youth ministry, I see smaller American churches, urban ministries, and the global church actually *engaging* in the lives of teenagers. And they're doing so in ways that reflect our redefined youth ministry roles.

Due to the perceived lack of resources, our brothers and sisters in these contexts have been "divinely forced" to utilize the whole community as they train up the "next generation." I've heard the lament as smaller churches or urban ministries long to hire a youth pastor or additional staff to serve teenagers. But I want to commend our co-laborers for their approach. The ways they're investing in teenagers are precisely what larger churches or megachurches want more of—more care from the whole church, more parental involvement, and a long-term view of faith development. The silos that many churches must tear down in order to bridge the generations and build relationships between them simply aren't a problem in those smaller contexts. They are, in fact, leading the resource-laden ministries in this respect.

After I'd finished speaking on this vision, a key leader in Latin America came up and hugged me, and then he whispered in my ear, "This is what the Latin church has been doing for years. You're right on. Thank you!" We should be thanking *you* for your faithful service and leadership—especially when you were told you were doing something wrong, that you needed larger crowds, fancier technology, flashier gizmos, or more "fun events" on your calendar. Please forgive our arrogance and speak up now more than ever so we can learn from your heritage.

After the assessment and waiting periods in my local church came to a close, we began hammering out the details regarding the kind of key leader we wanted to bring on to our team. Very soon, we determined a job title. We would hire a *Student Integration Pastor*.

What were our philosophical shifts as we redefined the role? In the big picture, the role we envisioned for our Student Integration Pastor was *to contribute to and collaborate with the broader church for meaningful, intentional, and mutual ways of integrating teenagers into the life of the church.* That's quite a mouthful. What do all of those polysyllabic words really mean?

In the beginning, we looked to the unique, God-given fingerprint of our church. As a part of the global church, God has invited our local church to make a unique contribution in the kingdom, and we wanted to remain faithful to that calling. For us, our Purple Cow (Seth Godin's infamously coined metaphor) was that this person had to be a ***third-culture person***, having the "mindset and will to love, learn, and serve, even in the midst of pain and discomfort." We were committed to bringing someone onto our team who could adapt to multiple cultures and contexts, work with a wide range of people, and be energized about melding two different cultures together while creating a third culture. We knew this "new way" would be uncomfortable and painful for our church members who were used to a generation of traditional youth ministry and perfectly comfortable with the way things were.

Next, we wanted to go headlong into an ***intergenerational approach*** to youth ministry. Since I was an Advisory Council member of Fuller Youth Institute, at that point our church had been digging into the Sticky Faith research for more than five years. We believe in it. Paul's words to young Timothy about the relationship between the older and younger generations deeply resonated with us.

Second Timothy 2:2 (NLT) is like a cheat sheet for how faith is passed from generation to generation. Paul compels his young disciple, *"You have heard me teach things that have been confirmed by many reliable witnesses. Now teach these truths to other trustworthy people who will be able to pass them on to others."* In other words, a symbolic baton should be passed from mentor to mentee who then, in turn, becomes a mentor for another. It's a simple equation. Jesus modeled the same powerful approach as he walked with 12 young men who became world changers. The power isn't found in the large crowds; it's found in the investment that's being made into a small group of believers who then turn their world upside down!

We dreamed our community would become a place that echoed Paul's words in 1 Timothy 4:12 (NLT), *"Don't let anyone think less of you because you are young. Be an example to all believers in what you say, in the*

> *We are no longer trying to shore up the areas that don't work. . . We now talk more about "the family."*
> — Lars Rood

way you live, in your love, your faith, and your purity."
Our lead pastor, Dave Gibbons, frequently says we are a church for the "next" generation, and our prayerful desire is that the youth will lead the church in many ways—in worship, prayer, evangelism, and care for the poor. These two Scriptures highlighted our vision for the Student Integration Pastor.

We put a stake in the ground by saying that mutual, intentional, and meaningful togetherness would be a distinguishing quality of our church. Yes, teenagers need age-appropriate gatherings and equipping, but this approach should be the exception, not the rule in terms of our thinking and calendar plans. We believe in using an age-appropriate version of the broader church vision and practical experience to help our teenagers make the transition into the whole church post-graduation. If the youth ministry's vision and practical experience are completely different from that of the whole church, then we're essentially giving our teenagers a bait-and-switch. No wonder they don't know how to choose a church, connect in the adult community, or translate their youth group experience once they exit our youth ministry bubble.

Along those lines, we determined that our student integration pastor would be ***collaborative and big picture.*** In all things, our youth ministry would look at ways the entire church was growing and developing, and then consider how that growth might intersect with our teenagers. Beyond collaboration between the youth ministry and the whole church, we must take a closer look at the families within the church as well. Every family has something to offer. We would look for those strengths, call them out, and invite our families to help us develop our teenagers. Far too often and for too long, the students' immediate families and their spiritual family have been downplayed in our efforts to create safe youth ministry havens for teenagers. We believe it takes a village to raise a child, and that village needs to be *much* larger than a siloed youth ministry.

We also identified that our Student Integration Pastor needed to be ***highly relational, not programmatic and segmented.*** In many churches, a disproportionate percentage of the youth pastor's time is invested into creating programs, not walking with people. What if we turned that ratio upside down?

I'll never forget the staff meeting where our lead pastor challenged us to get out of the office and spend more

We are beginning to think about the family and the partnership with them. This is especially important for a commuter church like ours.
— Keegan Lenker

time with our people. He said we weren't getting paid to build programs and sit in our offices. And then he charged us to spend 20+ hours of our work week with people. I remember shaking my head. *That's impossible,* I thought. It was impossible within the constructs I had built. In the years since that meeting, we've managed to turn things around. Now our team spends a great percentage of their time investing in people over programs. As we look to imitate Jesus' philosophy of ministry by spending time with people for maximum kingdom impact, our leaders are regularly asked, "Who are your 3, 12, and 30?" We are held accountable for walking with a few for maximum impact. Just as Jesus spent more time with the 30 than the crowds, poured his life into the 12 disciples, and brought Peter, James and John closest to him, so we are challenged to model that type of relational investment into the lives of a few.

The last primary characteristic of the Student Integration Pastor is that he or she should be a ***champion for teenagers.*** This person would be the lead banner-waver reminding our church of their responsibility of spiritually forming teenagers. He or she would educate, cast vision, and inspire the people in our community, making sure they know not only how incredible teenagers are, but also what they need to develop a lifelong faith. This person would also give a voice and hope to a generation in need of both.

Beyond Student Integration Pastor

Yes, we took great pains to evaluate the old and redefine the new role of our point leader. Yet by the very nature of the position, it was clear this transformation went way beyond a pastoral role. These changes would impact, infiltrate, and influence every person within our community. We weren't simply scoping out a new reality for the point leader; we were reimagining every person's role. So while this book is about redefining the role of the youth worker, it also implicates a necessary role change for everyone in the body of Christ.

We finished sketching out this position, and I couldn't help but believe everyone would be ecstatic about the changes. How could you not want to see this picture come to life? I was in for a rude awakening. Our skeptics wondered if this was just a trendy new title wrapped up in a slightly different package. Even some of my biggest fans would pull me down a dark hallway and whisper, "Come on, tell me the truth. This job is actually still a youth pastor, right?" Emphatically I would contend that there are some real differences in this new role: the focus, the time reallocation, the breadth of the people involved, and the ways we'll be talking about youth ministry in the future.
Somewhere down a dark hallway, I realized leading this change would be more difficult than I expected.

Questions to Consider

- What about the idea of "redefining the youth worker role" resonates with you?

- What are some of the unique characteristics about your context that will frame your changes?

- Specifically, what values or characteristics need to be redefined in your context?

- Where are these desirable characteristics already at work in your church?

Chapter Four

Leading Change

> *Where there is no vision, the people perish.*
> — Proverbs 29:18 (KJV)

> *Leadership is hard; get over it.*
> — Nancy Ortberg, Author of *Unleashing the Power of Rubber Bands: Lessons in Non-Linear Leadership*

Some days I really, really, really wish leadership were easier—and people weren't so difficult! There are some days when leading people is so hard that I want to turn off my alarm, roll over, pull the sheets up over my head, and let someone else make the hard decisions.

It's hard. I get it. Now, let's get over it.

Leadership isn't a right; it's a privilege and a calling from the Most High God. Leadership is a spiritual gift supernaturally given by God for the sake of his people.

I love the Old Testament story of Moses leading the Israelites out of slavery. I love the specific way God called Moses into leadership, aggressively responding to every excuse he gave of as to why God couldn't use him to lead a the million slaves out of the tyrannical hands of Pharaoh. Finally, they fled Pharaoh's grip and began their estimated two-week journey out of Egypt toward the Promised Land flowing with milk and honey. I love the big bang of the exodus, how the waters of the Red Sea miraculously parted before them and then swallowed up the enemy as they chased after the Israelites. I also love how God's chosen people stood breathlessly victorious on the opposite shore after watching how God protected and delivered them from Egypt. The first part of the story is powerful—filled with drama and promise and supernatural miracles. It's such a powerful reminder of the greatness of our God.

The next part of the story pains me. They wandered. They disobeyed God. They made idols, broke promises, and were incredibly cruel to each other and God's chosen leader. And an entire generation of Israelites was lost in the desert on the way to the Promised Land. I don't imagine they wanted to trade their names from "slaves" to "nomads."

And Moses, described as a servant of the Lord, died in the desert. His legacy is a mixed one filled with many excuses, undeniable courage, unfulfilled promises, heartbreaking disobedience, and powerful faith. In fact, in his "obituary" it says, *"There has never been another prophet in Israel like Moses, whom the LORD knew face to face"* (Deuteronomy 34:10, NLT). And, to me, one of the saddest verses of the Bible says, *"Then the LORD said to Moses, 'This is the land I promised on oath to Abraham, Isaac, and Jacob when I said, "I will give it to your descendants." I have now allowed you to see it with your own eyes, but you will not enter the land.'"* (Deuteronomy 34:4, NLT).

What went wrong? In part, Moses failed to lead change well.

Enter Joshua. Scripture says he was *"full of the spirit of wisdom"* (Deuteronomy 34:9, NLT). God promises Joshua he will lead the people into the Promised Land, and he will never abandon this young leader. God had gone before him. Then, he speaks a charge and blessing into Joshua's soul, filling him for the high task of leading through massive change:

> *"Be strong and courageous, for you are the one who will lead these people to possess all the land I swore to their ancestors I would give them. Be strong and very courageous. Be careful to obey all the instructions Moses gave you. Do not deviate from them, turning either to the right or to the left. Then you will be successful in everything you*

do. Study this Book of Instruction continually. Meditate on it day and night so you will be sure to obey everything written in it. Only then will you prosper and succeed in all you do. This is my command—be strong and courageous! Do not be afraid or discouraged. For the LORD your God is with you wherever you go." (Joshua 1:6-9, NLT)

You know the rest of the story: Joshua led the next generation of Israelites into the Promised Land. I find it interesting, though, that even in the midst of God's promise to Joshua, he was repeatedly commanded to be "strong and courageous." It's as if God wanted to give Joshua confidence that this change would come about, yet Joshua still needed God's strength and courage to fulfill the promise.

There are a few things I've learned to be true in leading any kind of change.

1. Systematic change takes a long time.
John Kotter says, "leaders typically fail to acknowledge that large-scale change can take years" (Kotter 1995, 2) The result? Stunted transformation. Why? Because change simply takes a long time. So the proper response of the leader should be to honor reality and stay the course.

Proverbs 21:5 is certainly a sobering verse about the role of long-term change. The wise author wrote, *"Good planning and hard work lead to prosperity, but hasty shortcuts lead to poverty."* Leading change demands planning and then working your plan over the long haul. I'm certain systemic change may be put in place within a year or less, but the lasting fruit of that change will bloom only after years of "steady plodding."

Brooklyn Lindsey is a youth worker I deeply respect. She's been in the process of leading change in her local context for several years now. I know the journey has often felt like two steps forward, one step back. This is the nature of the beast called "change." But she presses on in the vision God's given to her community. In the midst of those changes, she admits, "I still cross over back and forth from the traditional model to the new model, but the transitions are becoming easier to make." As she moves her people closer toward the vision's fulfillment, she makes concessions in order to honor their journey. Her leadership shows wisdom, patience, and love for the community God ordained her to lead.

Dr. Scott Cormode, Hugh De Pree Professor of Leadership Development at Fuller Theological Seminary, is an expert in organizational and leadership change.

He references the longevity of large-scale change by framing expectations for the leader: "Leaders have to fail people's expectations at a rate they can stand."

Ugh.

That statement reeks of disappointment, and failure, and pain. Yes, leadership is hard. Get over it.

On the flip side, Dr. Cormode's assessment braces me to know what to anticipate. It helps me as a leader to know meaningful change will bring about those difficult situations. And knowing is half the battle.

2. Leaders take people to places they don't want to go on their own, but places where they *need* to go.

When a leader sees a new way, he or she must take people to that new place. But when you take people to a new place, you're bound to experience resistance. My gut sense is that if you're not experiencing resistance, then you probably aren't leading change.

> *A change in structure will not be vibrant and living unless it is accompanied by a change in the environment.*
> — Paraphrase from Mark DeVries'
> *Sustainable Youth Ministry*

There is a difference between *leadership* and *management:*

> *Leaders step out into the future to discern what God is calling the congregation to do in the next chapter of its life. Managers are the voice of stability in the congregation (and therefore sensitive to measures of happiness or satisfaction); leaders are the voice of change in the congregation (and more sensitive to measures of purpose and faithfulness).* (Rendle 1998, 14)

If God has called you to lead a change in your community, you will need to be sensitive and thick-skinned at the same time.

Fuller Youth Institute asked youth workers who'd participated in past Sticky Faith Cohorts to share about the mistakes they'd made in leading change. The common responses were:

- Timing of the change—*When change happens is just as important as what changes are proposed.*

- Initiating too much change too soon—This can feel like whiplash if people aren't prepared to enter the change.

- Experimenting on the margins more—Instead of

making changes that affect everyone right away, experiment by implementing changes within smaller groups before increasing the impact.

- Pushing for change too fast or not fast enough— This is the never-ending challenge of knowing how hard to push and knowing when people need a breather.

Transition and change are scary. You don't need to convince me otherwise! Change begs identification of sacred cows, failures, and inherent dysfunctions; and it will require a longer transition period to go from the old to the new. This process is messy and time-consuming... and yet so freeing! Taking the risk to re-envision new ways will open up previously unnoticed possibilities that can then be recalibrated for even greater kingdom impact and influence.

When I began leading this change in our church, we received a boatload of resistance. Too many people assumed we didn't really care about youth ministry anymore. We experienced a surprising amount of skepticism as some people thought we were merely creating a trendy title or tweaking programmatic elements. It was painful, and I didn't want to "get over" how hard it was to lead during that time. I wanted to shout obscenities to my critics and then wrestle these skeptics into a submission hold, WWE style. Honestly, I think I cried every day that summer because our people didn't "get it" and they made sure to communicate their displeasure. If I hadn't known and believed with all of my heart that I was obeying a prompting from God, I probably would have quit and gone back to Egypt instead of pressing forward toward the land God promised us.

So, how do we handle resistance? Dr. Scott Cormode offers some gentle yet strong counsel as to how we can lead change well by recalibrating our expectations with these thoughts on handling resistance.

First, expect resistance. It means people care and they are engaged. Have you ever considered people don't always resist change? Ronald Heifetz insists, "People don't resist change, they resist loss." When we talk about loss, we are talking about grief. And in order to properly grieve the loss(es) change brings with it, people need to work through the five stages of grief: denial, anger, depression, bargaining, and (*finally*) acceptance.

If you're like me and you need to lose some weight, are you adverse to that change in your body? Absolutely not. I'd love to feel healthier and see a thinner me in the mirror. Give me the magical pill! But if you tell me I'll have to remove processed foods, red wine, and sweet treats from my diet, and limit eating out in order to get there . . . that's another conversation! Tell me I have to run five miles a day in order to reach my goal weight? I'd rather be fat.

I resist the loss of the foods I love and the pain of starting a regular exercise routine. Yet I still want to experience the positive changes in my body. Funny or not, a little grief process needs to take place in order for me to accept the losses associated with those necessary changes that eventually lead to weight loss. The resistance I experience isn't about the change; it's about what will be lost as a result. (Interestingly enough, while writing this book, I made a decision to embrace this change and lost weight! My initial resistance to the losses of certain foods and inactivity eventually moved to the acceptance stage, and then change finally happened.)

Second, talk in terms people care about. Ultimately, we all care about the same thing: seeing our teenagers walking with Jesus for a lifetime and making a difference in the kingdom. The desired end result is the same. The means is what's been questioned. As you listen to people's fears, find those places where you care about the same things and create new terms together.

Third, change can mean loss or change can meet a longing. Your church's elders may be afraid that redefining the role of the youth worker means you no longer care about teenagers at your church. Parents may be afraid this change will cost them more spiritual engagement with their kids. Teenagers may fear having to sit through mind-numbingly boring church services in exchange for their students-only service. But a change in vision may also meet a longing. A single mom longs for her son to have father figures in his life, so integrating him into the life of the church helps meet a deep longing in her heart. Empty nesters long for their nests to be filled with energy again, so an invitation to participate in teenagers' lives may call out a latent desire. Parents may be struggling with their pubescent daughter's choices and defiance of their authority, and the church has now created value in gathering the village to support them through this time.

Lastly, Dr. Cormode defines vision as "a shared story of a future hope." This is my favorite description of vision because foretelling the future and desired outcome must be done together in storytelling. Dave Gibbons, the lead pastor and my boss at Newsong, says vision must emerge out of relationship. More likely than not, the vision God has given to your church includes your vision, but it's not exclusive to what you see. Listening to the stories of your people will enlarge your future direction.

Proverbs talks about people "perishing" without vision. Vision is a big deal. We die without it. And I'd dare to say that the 50 percent of teenagers who walk away from Christ and his church are perishing, in part, because of our lack of vision in youth ministry.

As our church redefined the role as a leader who was all about integration, relationships, collaboration, and cheerleading, we saw living examples of this vision already at work in our church. For instance, Linda, a mom of five kids, grasped the vision and started a Bible study with two high school girls, two college girls, two young adults, and two moms. Our church's worship leader, DK, made intentional efforts to mentor up-and-coming worship leaders in our high school and college ministries. One of our college students, Victor, began serving in our children's ministry and then recruited a ton of his friends to join him. And as they poured themselves into our youngest ones, they were surprised to find their own faith being nurtured by spiritual mothers and fathers in our community.

So as a team, we carefully identified, crafted, articulated, and told a handful of stories like these again and again as if we were broken records. There was a time period when I literally told my team they weren't allowed to speak in public, send an email, lead a training session, or open their mouths without sharing a story about our future hope. And the vision started to catch on.

Another story we shared repeatedly was about Sonsern, a young man who started served in our middle school ministry when he was a college sophomore. He built a trusting relationship with one of the middle school students who then invited Sonsern to his birthday party. Sonsern saw this as an opportunity to bless this student and get to know his family. Even though Sonsern had a final coming up, he made the time to go and said yes to the invitation. Sonsern bought a birthday gift for the student, and he played video games with the student and his friends during the party. But he also took the initiative to engage the student's parents. He introduces himself as their son's small group leader and proceeded to tell them about his major. The parents spoke about their own college days and majors, and how what they studied was totally irrelevant to their current careers.

The parents began a relationship with Sonsern as they saw the positive influence he was having on their teenage son. Sonsern continued to be invited to major events in the middle school student's life, and he became a regular at the family's house. Even though Sonsern isn't from the area, he built a very close relationship with this family and felt at home at Newsong. He even stayed in the area during a few of his school breaks in order to celebrate holidays with his student's family.

As the time drew near for Sonsern to graduate from college, the student's father connected Sonsern with a business friend who offered him an internship. Fast-forward a couple of years: one of our church elders and her husband mentored Sonsern, and he ended up living with them for a time. Sonsern was a living story of our future hope of collaborative, intergenerational, mutual relationships throughout our church.

Sonsern's story illustrates a point I made earlier in this chapter: the establishment of vision takes years. One reason for this delay might be the fact that, as Bill Hybels says, "vision leaks." No matter how compelling your vision, the complexity of real life will cause whatever vision you communicate to people to practically evaporate from their minds. Leaders must continually refill people's "vision buckets" because life will poke holes in the bottoms of those buckets, allowing the vision you've so carefully communicated to slowly drain away (Hybels 2008, ch. 13). In fact, some leadership gurus say vision leaks every 28 days. I'd argue it probably drains faster whenever large-scale change is in play. Therefore, our shared stories of future hope have to be communicated over and over and over and over and over again.

Priority of Communication

My guess is most everyone who has led people through an important change can testify to the truth that communication is of vital importance. Yet it's also probably the area where we tend to fail with gusto. In order to continually refill people's vision buckets, we need to improve our communication abilities.

One youth worker faulted herself for communicating more about the "what" than the "why." However, this is a leader's natural response because people tend to ask more "what" questions even though they're actually looking for answers to their "why" questions. We must keep in mind that the "what" questions will answer themselves with greater ease when the "why" question is repeatedly answered from a variety of angles.

Another youth worker affirmed that communication was "the most crucial element of leading change," saying it was imperative to ask people to clarify what had been communicated to them. Too often we think we're communicating in clear, simple language; yet what's being received is something altogether different. Upon hearing the audience's perception, a leader can better understand what people are taking away from the

> *It is easy for those of us on staff to forget that we've been living with an idea for months or years, and we often expect our parents and congregation to "buy in" after a one-hour meeting or a few weeks. This is just not realistic. Change is hard. It takes time. It's messy, but it's worth it.*
> — Alan Mercer

message. Feedback will help you discern whether or not your message is accomplishing the desired intention:

- Am I communicating the heart of the vision?
- Which words or images are tripping them up?
- What energizes them for the future?
- What parts are too confusing or overcompli cated for the listener?
- How can I hone the message into smaller, bite-sized pieces?
- What ideas and stories are resonating with different groups of people?

This is active listening in its truest form. The hard pill to swallow is that perception is reality. So if you're communicating that you're planning to integrate teenagers into the main worship service every weekend, but people hear that you're canceling the youth group, then you have a communication problem. The perception may be wrong, but it's reality for those who are deducing your message.

Questions to Consider

- Who do you expect will resist different changes? Why?

- What is your community longing for?

- Can you identify two to three shared stories of a future hope that can guide you toward your vision?

Chapter Five

360-Degree Leadership

> *If God has given you leadership ability, take the responsibility seriously.*
> — Romans 12:8 (NLT)

> *We're trained to "get stuff done," but sometimes the only thing that is getting done when we go for it, all at once, is our sustainability as a human being, as a life-giver, as someone created in the image of God. We find ourselves buried and wondering where ministry lost its beauty.*
> —Brooklyn Lindsey, Youth Pastor
> Highland Park Church of the Nazarene,
> Lakeland, FL

The needs of ministry are endless. People to meet with. Sermons to write. Special events to plan. Emails to answer. Parents to equip. New team members to recruit. Staff meetings to attend. Difficult conversations to engage. Meetings to plan and lead. Prayer to cover it all.

Now throw in leading change on top of it all . . . and I

sense you want to throw this book across this room or post a nasty review on Amazon. Please don't. There is hope.

One of the reasons why reimagining the role of the youth worker is so vital is that when we try to live underneath such a large pile of expectations, something's eventually gotta give. Lifelong youth ministry champion Mark DeVries gives a sobering perspective on the realities we experience with this way of thinking:

> *The superstar syndrome always creates larger problems, not the least of which is removing the family, the elders, the deacons and other concerned adults from the lives of teenagers and replacing them with a new "youth ghetto" in which the rest of the church simply lets the youth minister take care of the kids.* (DeVries 2008, 50)

Unintentionally or not, have we made ourselves superstars? Have we created a system of insanity that allows us to do everything when we were never intended to provide for all the spiritual needs (not to mention physical, emotional, social, and intellectual needs) of teenagers?

Years ago Bill Hybels gave a talk during a Willow
Creek children's ministry conference on becoming a
stronger 360-degree leader, one who can lead well in all
directions. In no uncertain terms, he masterfully walked
through the importance of self-leadership, leading up
(your boss), leading laterally (your peers), and leading
down (your team and followers). I've probably listened
to that message a dozen times, and it still challenges
me—particularly in the area of self-leadership. (A video
of his talk is available at http://www.willowcreekevents.
org.uk/media/video/childrens-ministry-team-sessions-
leadership-1/.)

Self-Leadership

We've all read the media headlines and have personal
connections to leaders who've collapsed internally as
the result of self-leadership failure. No one intends
to implode or fail; but knowing our depravity, it will
happen to us if we neglect the care of our souls.

Hybels convincingly argues that 50 percent of our
leadership efforts need to be allocated toward leading
ourselves. FIFTY PERCENT! Now, that doesn't mean
we should spend 20 hours of our 40-hour work weeks
"developing" ourselves. But it does have serious
implications for the ways we discipline our thoughts,
care for our souls, and guard our hearts.

I'm sure you've heard it said that leadership is lonely. In my early leadership years, I thought that was a ridiculous cop-out for leaders who weren't intentionally cultivating community in their lives. I used to think loneliness was a leader's excuse. In fact, I not-so-secretly questioned leaders who expressed their feelings of loneliness, thinking, *You made your bed; now sleep in it.* Much to my embarrassment, I now know that experiencing a degree of loneliness in leadership is not only real, but it's inevitable if you are truly leading people.

How do you care for your soul and take responsibility for your soul's health?

Gilbert Rendle writes, "The first thing leaders can do is to relieve themselves of the pressure to come up with the perfect 'answer' to an uncertain future that will keep all parties in the congregation 'happy.' . . . Happiness and satisfaction are very often measures of the status quo" (Rendle 1998, 13).

Scripture is full of appeals for us to care for and lead ourselves, and it provides some good examples for us

> *The best gift you can give your church and people is a healthy, energized, passionate, fully surrendered self.*
> — Bill Hybels

to follow as well. King Solomon, the wisest man to ever live, wrote, *"Above all else, guard your heart, for everything you do flows from it"* (Proverbs 4:23, NIV). In the New Testament Jesus warns, *"The thief's purpose is to steal and kill and destroy. My purpose is to give [my sheep] a rich and satisfying life"* (John 10:10, NLT). And throughout the Gospels we frequently see Jesus retreating to "lonely places" to pray.

I'm not sure what it takes for you stay centered, energized, present, engaged, rested, and passionate in life. However, I am quite sure no matter what that activity might be, it's crucial to your ability to lead change without killing your soul in the process. No change is worth compromising your soul or leadership influence. God's Word affirms your value by asking, *"What do you benefit if you gain the whole world but lose your own soul?"* (Mark 8:36, NLT). Being a superstar leader isn't worth much if it means sacrificing your soul, nor is implosion an inevitable result of leadership.

There's no formula for leading yourself well, but as human beings there is some common ground we share for soul care.

- ***Prayer and Scripture Reading.*** I asked my spiritual director, Mindy, if these two spiritual practices were really essential for Christ-followers, or if other practices could be substituted for them. Mindy may have laughed at my silly question, but I've never forgotten her answer. She said, "Prayer is the language of our relationship with God, and the Bible is the fullest expression of God's spoken word to us. So, no, you cannot connect with God without engaging those two disciplines." Point taken.

• **Silence and Solitude.** The late Brennan Manning was often quoted as saying, "be very wary of the person who cannot be alone with God." Rhythms involving daily, weekly, monthly, and annual times to be quiet and alone with God are so helpful for our perspective and our connection with the only Audience we must please.

• **Sabbath and Rest.** In a world that's wired and continuously connected, I'm still surprised by our inability to take time off from the tyranny of the urgent and simply rest. I love John Ortberg's validation of rest when he says, "Perhaps the single most spiritual thing you could do right now is . . . take a nap" (Ortberg 1997, 50). Yes and amen.

• **Energy.** Who and what energizes and de-energizes you? Be mindful of the attention you're giving to each area. When we are leading ourselves well, we are prioritizing our attention to the people and things that give us energy.

- *Learners.* You've heard the old adage "you can only take people as far as you've gone yourself." This is especially true for leaders. We have to be relentless learners, endless sponges, hungry readers, overly curious seekers, and pursuing mentors. Gilbert Rendle encouraged this form of self-leadership by saying, "Rather than do, leaders are at times called to learn—and to teach others what they are learning" (Rendle 1998, 149). If we believe that God's Word to us is almost always for the other (an idea that's attributed to Dietrich Bonhoeffer), then we must be postured to receive that Word through a learning spirit.

Take a moment right now and consider: In order for you to lead yourself well, what are the unique requirements of your soul? Name them.
It is within our self-leadership that we are able to pay attention and be responsive to the whispers of the Holy Spirit in our midst.

Evaluate your self-leadership through the lens of these piercing questions (taken from Bill Hybels' "360-Degree Leadership" message):

- Is my calling sure?
- Is my vision clear?

- Is my passion burning hot?
- Is my character fully submitted to Christ?
- Are my fears at bay?
- Is my psychological baggage affecting my current decisions?
- Are my ears open to the Spirit?
- Is my pace sustainable?
- Is my heart increasing or decreasing?

If you're human and honest in your responses, the Holy Spirit will surely speak to ways you can improve your self-leadership. Perhaps these questions will even save your soul from the internal collapse we all want to avoid.

As you discover and continually rediscover how you need to lead yourself, my prayer for you echoes the

What, then, is the role of congregational leaders? It is to be faithful to the journey—to the challenge, the experimentation, the trial and error of ministry in a culture of change. And it is to be responsive.
— Gilbert R. Rendle, *Leading Change in the Congregation*

words of the prophet Isaiah, *"The LORD will guide you continually, giving you water when you are dry and restoring your strength. You will be like a well-watered garden, like an ever-flowing spring"* (Isaiah 58:11, NLT). It is possible—in fact, it is God's desire—for you to be filled with life in all seasons of leadership. Take your self-leadership seriously. The kingdom will be fuller with your influence!

Leading Up

As Hybels went on to describe the full spectrum of leadership, he assessed that 25 percent of your leadership focus needs to be on leading your boss. I think youth ministry has subversively taught us to avoid our bosses at all costs because an interaction likely means we've done something wrong! Or maybe we're afraid of or disgusted by church politics, so we steer clear of the "business" side of ministry. Or perhaps we long to stay out of the line of fire with our lead pastors so we can continue doing our own thing. *Au contraire.* Mark DeVries shakes up our destructive patterns: "By joining a church staff, a youth worker automatically steps onto the political playing field. And the one who holds firmly to 'I don't play politics' often leads a ministry that is dramatically underfunded" (DeVries 2008, 28). Beyond being underfunded, not leading our bosses will cause our reimagined vision to go unnoticed, underappreciated, undervalued, and more.

As youth workers, we have to get past our insecurities and the fear of our bosses. We must recognize that in order to break the cycle of isolated youth ministry, we have to step into higher-level leadership. This is especially true when your vision for change doesn't originate from your boss. Brooklyn Lindsey has referred to this perplexing task as "changing from the middle." While it is certainly possible to lead ministry-specific change apart from your boss's engagement, it will be much more difficult to do. There is definitely a perceived obstacle in the field of youth ministry that youth workers are unable to influence any decisions beyond their own domain. But I believe much of our perception is related to our ability to lead up. If systemic change is what you're after, engaging senior leadership will be required.

How successful you are in leading change is directly correlated to the amount of support your new vision receives from both your boss and the lead pastor. Their level of trust and confidence in you matters tremendously. Your ability to educate and inspire your boss will determine the ease of the changes. Learning to speak your boss's language will allow your message to go much further than your sole voice. Then when criticism comes, and it will, having a boss who has your back will go a long way. Relationship and influence are inextricably linked. Build the relationship with your boss and the momentum will positively shift.

When we began making these shifts within our church, I realized the need to have our lead pastor's ear more. So I requested a 15-minute meeting with him and asked the question, "What would be most helpful for you as we go about leading this change?" He was thrilled to answer and gave me fantastic insights into how he is best educated, inspired, and informed, as well as which means of communication he appreciates and prefers. Those 15 minutes saved me a lot of guessing and subsequent missteps, and they tremendously improved our working relationship.

After having our lead pastor's heart and ear over the past few years, I've realized something even more: Lead pastors deal with a level of leadership complexity that I will never fully understand. The amount of criticism, seemingly competing agendas, difficult decisions, and spiritual intensity that surrounds them is beyond my scope and understanding.

A few years ago, one of my dearest friends was starting a church, and she and her husband would be the lead pastors. As they began piecing together the vision God was giving them for their city, they realized the weight of leadership only they would carry. As a result, she went back to every lead pastor she'd ever served under and specifically thanked them for their impactful influence on her life. But she didn't stop there. She also apologized for reluctantly following them at times by judging their decisions, undermining their leadership, or disrespecting them in any way. God illuminated for her just how significant the act of leading up really is and how much we tend to underperform in this area of leadership.

Leading Laterally

As you care for your soul and work to bring your lead pastor onto your team, actively engaging those who will be directly affected by the change is critically important—including but not limited to, other ministries in your church. Hybels advocates that 20 percent of your leadership influence should be directed toward your peer group.

As we began leading change at Newsong, I increased the amount of face time with our children's pastor, college pastor, creative arts leaders, mom's ministry leaders, and other influencers throughout our church. My goal? Build relationships with those who would either allow this vision to become a reality or keep us quarantined as a siloed youth ministry. Hybels says the key to lateral leadership is servanthood. As I increased my presence and participation in their areas of influence, shared stories of future hope, answered questions, and listened to their fears, it clarified for me how my team and I could lead the change well.

John Kotter's ideology is that developing a guiding coalition of peers will enable you to "develop a shared commitment to renewal" (Kotter 1995, 2). Without that team, your efforts will either be stunted or fail entirely. But together, the team raises our effectiveness and is called to a higher level. Together, we all advance in the mission God has called us to both individually and corporately.

Leading Down

If you've been tallying the percentages, you'll notice Hybels' 360-degree leadership approach leaves only five percent of your energy focused on leading down. What a paradigm shift! However, that five percent is imperative as we consider the parents, teenagers, and volunteers who look to us for leadership. When the other 95 percent of your leadership is directed in the right areas, the final five percent is ultra-concentrated and flows strongly.

Leading down is about coming face to face with the chaos change brings. Gilbert Rendle writes:

The fact is that few, if any, of us are anxious to walk into chaos, where answers are hidden and rules are unknown. Chaos is not welcome in our personal lives, marriages, or friendships, and certainly not in our congregations. In fact, one of the issues leaders need to attend to in times of deep change is the management of the fear (their own and the congregation's) of having little control and few answers. (Rendle 1998, 95)

Chaos and change and the need for control are intertwined with one another. The higher the degree of change and chaos, the higher one's perceived need for control. Leaders love to control things. Yet I've learned you cannot control people and love people at the same time. (Shout-out to Mike Park for this truth.) You can either love them OR you can control them.

If Scripture is telling the truth that *"perfect love drives*

Keeping the change at the forefront of priority has been pivotal for me and for the leadership here. The consistency of language and speaking about it has helped to create an environment of willingness rather than feelings of "more work."
—Keegan Lenker

out fear" (1 John 4:18, NIV), then perhaps there's no higher calling than to love our people well through their fears. I've seen over and over again that loving people to the other side of fear provides a crucible for deep spiritual formation that's well beyond vision and change. After all, this entire change is about people. Nothing else matters more.

May you never sacrifice loving people for the sake of fulfilling your God-given vision. Never.

Questions to Consider

- What percentage of your leadership energy are you currently directing toward these four areas?

  - Self-Leadership

  - Leading Up

  - Leading Laterally

  - Leading Down

- Where and how are you neglecting 360-degree leadership? Be specific.

- What are two to three immediate changes you can make to improve your 360-degree leader ship?

Chapter Six

Regular Reassessment

> *Teach us to number our days,*
> *so we may gain a heart of wisdom.*
> — Psalm 90:12 (NIV)

> *It is the premature victory celebration that kills*
> *momentum.*
> — John Kotter, "Leading Change"

Our church is now two years into our new vision, and we continually need to work at deepening that vision's reality in big and small ways. Our current practices are not where we eventually hope to end up. We still have a ways to go for our vision to become reality. You may think once you make the "big changes," most of the hard work is completed. Wrong. But I wish you were right. Diligent, intentional, and thoughtful leadership is still required. Leaders must regularly reassess what's working as a result of the changes, what's not working, what still needs attention, and how people are responding to the changes. The vision doesn't end with implementation; it ends with saturation and acceptance.

The first year after we hired our Student Integration Pastor was filled with exhilarating highs, epic failures, and continual re-evaluation. Maybe my memory serves me wrong, but after the initial changes were made, I don't remember receiving a lot of criticism and resistance. Perhaps it was because those who didn't want to be a part of the change simply left the church. (These folks were in the minority.)

But those who stuck around did so for a few reasons. First, they knew we were serious since we were actually implementing changes. Hiring the Student Integration Pastor was proof we meant business. Second, I believe the critics felt heard and cared for throughout the process. Now, it took lots of patience, self-control, and humble apologies for not listening well the first time; but it served us well on the other side of the change. Lastly, I think people just shut up and waited to see if this experiment would actually work. I'm a believer that time and truth walk hand in hand. So skeptics and advocates alike waited to see what truth would emerge from the decisions we made.

The most dramatic changes we made were in the high school ministry. Immediately there was an influx of energy and passion from some key, influential teenagers who had some firsthand, developmentally specific experiences within an intergenerational context. (These

> We recognize the movement forward is
> slow, but our willingness to succeed and fail
> together is really helpful for all of us.
> — Keegan Lenker

included a family trip to Malawi, Africa, a student leadership training conference, and a YWAM summer training camp.) A number of those teenagers caught the vision and were beyond excited to be a part of the larger church. They eagerly received the invitation for more adults in their lives and to be more integrated into the broader church. They were amped to speak into the design of their ministry. Our high schoolers were enthusiastic about leaving behind the generic programming for customized experiences and greater unity with our church.

However, within a few months, the honeymoon period ended, and our high school students were disappointed there was no weekly gathering just for them. They still understood the vision, but we'd underestimated their need to belong to each other. They felt like the Israelites who left Egypt victoriously only to be brought out into the desert. Complaining and deferred hope overshadowed the vision. The Promised Land didn't come fast enough. We thought a sense of belonging within the whole church would be enough for them. It wasn't. It was a serious low for our leadership team as we perceived this as a step backward. However, we were committed not to sacrifice our teenagers for the sake of the vision. So we compromised and made a shift. Two steps forward. One step back. (More on this in the Epilogue.)

The words of Gilbert R. Rendle rang true in my ears:

> *The role of the leader is to pay attention long enough and not run off to fix something. It is to help people confront their pain, disappointments, and anxieties without diminishing them but also without being overwhelmed by them. It is to help people dream dreams of alternate possibilities that provide direction and energy. It is to help people escape the boxes of their assumptions and learned behavior so that deep change is not subverted by old rules. And, perhaps most importantly, it is to help hold people in the wilderness of their experience, the chaos of not knowing what comes next until it comes.* (Rendle 1998, 99)

My tendency is to fix and relieve pain. Crucial conversations are not my favorite kinds of conversations. People-pleasing is my default. Yet these traits are far from helpful in the process of change. Regardless of my preferences, we once again found ourselves paying attention to the words and the emotions behind the words. We disciplined ourselves not to fix every problem with a bandage or promise a solution we couldn't deliver. We invited our people into the long-term dream. And we prayed . . . a lot. We worked for a both/and approach to meeting the felt needs of our teenagers and their families, while staying true to the course God had marked out for us.

During that first year we also found ourselves training our youth ministry volunteers and key leaders from other ministries (paid and volunteer) on the reality of youth culture and our vision. I've found people are more attentive to your words when you've moved from vision/theory into reality/practice. There's an element of putting your money where your mouth is that's inspiring and intriguing to people who are skeptical about your vision.

One of the core principles in Jim Collins's infamous leadership book, *Good to Great,* is "disciplined thought plus disciplined action" makes greatness possible (Collins 2001). Creating a plan is important. Doing something and not getting stuck is critical. Following the plan is where the magic happens. You cannot have one without the other and expect the vision to miraculously materialize on its own.

We could have been much better about our disciplined thought and action that first year. In hindsight, we were much too reactionary. Honestly, I think we were simply tired after implementing so many changes and fleshing them out as best we could. We'd reached our limit.

During the second year, we started to find our groove. People were no longer questioning the viability of a Student Integration Pastor. Other leaders began considering the value teenagers could bring to their ministry spheres. Parents changed their expectations about the role of the youth ministry and stopped comparing it to their own youth group days. Student involvement in their schools and our church became much broader and deeper than it had been a couple of years before. Year two incurred far less resistance than the first one, and everyone was breathing a bit easier. Still, having disciplined thought and action leaves much to be desired.

The two tendencies in regular reassessment are (1) to over-evaluate, and (2) to under-evaluate. I am a master at both. When you over-evaluate, you end up spending all of your time critiquing and measuring your activity, leaving less and less time for actual action. When you under-evaluate, you miss out on a wealth of learning, repeat your mistakes (which leads us back to that definition of *insanity*), forget to celebrate big wins, and so much more. So how do we regularly evaluate the changes in a healthy way?

Rhythms of Evaluation

Determine some healthy rhythms by which to evaluate your ministry. Logical rhythms could include:

- Evaluating staff (volunteer and paid) at the end of every ministry year

- Debriefing after retreats, camps, or key events

- Assessing at the "end" (for example, at the end of December, at the end of the school year, at the end of the fiscal year, and at the end of the summer)

- Creating monthly reports that cite metric updates

A handful of rhythms should provide enough touchpoints for your team to be regularly "in the know" as to the state of the ministry.

Create Metrics

You have to determine what you're measuring. Define what success means to you, and this must include both qualitative and quantitative means. In matters of the soul and spiritual formation, it is difficult to quantify growth. But we must attempt to do so. Determine a few areas you want to measure. If you choose to measure more, you'll find yourself constantly in a state of measuring instead of "disciplined action." Quantifiable metrics must be able to be objectively measured: you did it or you didn't; you reached the goal or you didn't.

Art of Storytelling

Evaluating progress through the means of qualitative storytelling is one of the most life-giving and colorful ways you can share about progress and roadblocks. There is nothing like a story to communicate the values and life-change occurring, while also engaging our emotional center. Determine quantifiable ways you will use qualitative storytelling to provide assessment in your context.

Consider these ideas:

• Share a story of progress or success every time you have access to a public platform (staff meeting, Sunday service, parent meeting, video, social media post).

• Send a monthly e-blast to parents and volunteers including a picture along with the story.

• Create a weekly post for your blog or website which includes an interview or first-person story from someone who's life is being positively affected by the change.

• Forward encouraging calls, emails, and social media posts to your staff, your boss, or other key leaders.

• Whenever you meet with your boss, be ready to share a story or two about where the vision is at work in your midst.

• Redesign your website to prioritize the sharing these kinds of stories as a main feature.

• Start a social media page/account for the primary purpose of sharing stories of transformation.

• Capture one story every week of a parent, student, community leader, congregation member who's displaying what you're aiming for in your ministry.

Storytelling needs to be ongoing, but creating some mechanisms and habits will increase the ease and effectiveness of this ever-important task. One of my co-workers astutely notes, "What we celebrate is what we value." Therefore, as we tell these kinds of stories, we indirectly yet powerfully communicate what we value (and what we do not). Your words as a leader are weighty. Use them well.

When you combine the hard data of quantifiable metrics with artfully told stories, assessment can be truly helpful.

Matthew DePrez, a member of our Sticky Faith Cohort (2010), shared a beautiful example about the power of storytelling in assessing change. We were given an assignment by Dr. Cormode to write two "success stories" about students in our ministry. Matthew writes how the experience was so captivating and then the idea grew and spread. But it didn't stop there:

> *This is where we had the idea to take these "stories" one step further. In June we met as an adult leadership team, and each small group leader wrote one story about a student in their small group. It wrecked the small group leaders. Then we started wondering what would happen if students defined their own stories of life change? What if every student attending our program took time to write a story of future hope? And what would happen if they shared those stories of future hope with each other? It got us really excited!! In July, while our students were attending our annual summer camp, we made it a reality. Students took time to write their own stories of future hope and shared them with their peers. We had*

students committing to go into full-time ministry, leading other friends to Christ, and bringing their unchurched families to our church. The students dreamed bigger than I ever imagined!!

We've decided to center everything we do as a student ministry around these stories of future hope for 2012. It will become the foundation for each student that attends our program.

Stories can be powerful agents to transform us. According to Dr. Cormode, "People do not grab onto a plan, nor do they assent to abstract beliefs. That does not change them. Instead, people are transformed when they participate in a story—one that sets them on a trajectory . . . Participating in a story allows a person to imagine their way to change" ("A Shared Story of Future Hope," *The Next Faithful Step* blog, Fuller Theological Seminary).

As we assess how far we've come and how far we have yet to go, stories will likely be our closest companions. They will serve as a thermometer reading of our emotional temperature, measuring our excitement and fear.

Feedback Loop

There needs to be mechanisms and creative spaces in place for others to provide feedback. Keeping an open dialogue will be your friend as you evaluate the highs and lows of navigating change.

- Create a short-term, volunteer "Leading Change" team made up of people representing a wide cross section of your church, and ask them to go through this process with you.

- Offer a formal invitation for feedback at the end of every email.

- Share your cell phone number and any other helpful contact information.

- Design a brief, focused survey for teenagers and parents that captures real and felt needs. Be sure to share the results and learnings with the participating group. Make it optional to answer any open-ended questions or include their names on the survey.

- Host a breakfast or dessert with a specific audience, all for the purpose of listening to people and praying together.

- Make space after gatherings to be present and receive input.

- Strategically be present at gatherings where you need to be available for different groups of people.

This list of suggestions is far from exhaustive, but it can certainly point you in the right direction in terms of how to evaluate how things are going after you've made the big change. Guard your heart as you continue to move forward in creating a new culture. The apostle Paul reminds us of our calling not to lose heart or get weary while doing what is good. The work you are doing is undeniably hard, but it is also good. Stay the course and use the power of assessment to guide you toward your goal. *"At just the right time we will reap a harvest of blessing if we don't give up"* (Galatians 6:9, NLT).

Questions to Consider

- Do you tend to over-evaluate or under-evaluate your ministry?

- What are specific ways you can regularly assess the changes you make?

Epilogue

The Current Reality—Two Years Later

It's often easier to talk in more general terms about vision than about the hard work of seeing that vision become a reality. Our church has been increasingly moving into the new reality of our vision for the past two years. Therefore, I thought it would be good to end this little book with an honest reflection about what's been happening since we hired our Student Integration Pastor, Mike Park. I asked Mike to write from his "in the trenches" experiences. I pray his thoughts offer you some hopeful optimism regarding how far we've come and how much further we have yet to go . . .

When I first read the job description for the student integration pastor at Newsong, two thoughts crossed my mind. First, I knew the leadership had put a lot of thought and vision into the direction the church wanted to go regarding the youth ministry. The job title alone was ambitious but timely—this was exactly what those of us involved in youth ministry have been talking about for years. My second thought was "Are they really serious about doing it?" The answer to that second question was clearly YES, and two years later I'm pleased to say it is still true.

Earlier in this book, April walked you through principles for leading change that have been essential for us these last two years. When I first started as the Student Integration Pastor, I found myself doing a lot of explaining and a lot of listening. Explanation was important because very few people who weren't directly connected to our youth ministry knew what "student integration" meant. Casual introductions and hallway conversations became opportunities to share vision for an intergenerational ministry that helps teenagers be lifelong followers of Jesus Christ. I did a lot of listening, as well. Listening to God and listening to our people was the most important way for us to know how to navigate the resistance and course corrections that inevitably come with leading change.

One of the first shifts we made in our student ministries two years ago was a move from a high school-specific program on Sunday mornings to high school students attending our main worship service. The strategy and rationale behind that change was solid: we value intergenerational worship and community, and we want our teenagers to be an integral part of our Sunday morning gatherings. It all looked great on paper. As we explained it to our people, it was a great push toward our vision and what we felt like the church should look like. After several months, we realized that in a church with a few thousand people, it became difficult for our teenagers to feel a sense of belonging and community with one another. They felt lost in the crowd. New students had a difficult time connecting with us. Incoming freshmen nearly drowned in the change.

After hearing from God and from our people, we decided to make a course correction by having a high school-specific gathering on the first three Sundays of the month, and then the students would attend the main worship service on the last Sunday of the month. We were still committed to the vision and strategy, but the execution of that vision and strategy was different than what we'd originally planned. We are slowly moving forward toward intergenerational worship but it's taking longer than we anticipated. Part of that pace is also related to our creative experiences team working with our teenagers to create a service that is inclusive of them.

Another shift we've made at Newsong that's perhaps unique is giving our leaders permission—actually a mandate!—to focus on the few. Traditional models of ministry pour the most resource investment (time, financial, energy) into the largest events or programs, but often that's where you see the least amount of return. We're learning from Jesus' example of investing in the "3 and the 12" in order to see the most impact. He poured his life into a small number of people and saw a world-changing return. Our church's leadership actually holds me to the value of investing deeply in the few with the belief that discipleship happens best when we walk with others and see 2 Timothy 2:2 in full effect. Investing more of our resources into a few is a game-changing practice.

What I've learned in the past two years is that leading change as a student integration pastor means knowing what God is doing in my church and finding the best way for teenagers and families to be an integral part of what he is doing. At Newsong, one of our core principles comes from John 5:19—Jesus only did what he saw the Father doing. My role, then, is to highlight what God is doing among teenagers, in other ministries at our church, within families, at the local schools, and beyond, finding the best ways to connect, engage, and champion the movement of God together.

There's a temptation as the leader, especially in youth ministry, to think that the entire vision rests on me alone. When I started in this position, I felt the pressure to reinvent every aspect of the way we do youth ministry across the board. After all, shouldn't a ministry with a vision for student integration and being led by a student integration pastor look completely different? But that line of thinking falls into the same trap of trying to build a better youth ministry, rather than seeing the whole church as a place for meaningful relationships and spiritual formation for teenagers and families. Instead of innovative programming that specifically targets student integration, we work on making everything we do part of our student integration vision. As much as possible, we ask, "How can adults be involved in what teenagers are doing?" and "How can teenagers be involved in what adults are doing?" We believe we are better together than we are apart.

I can confidently say that all of Newsong (leaders, parents, adults, teenagers, pastor, and everyone in between) is invested in some way in what happens with middle schoolers and high schoolers. There is incredible collaboration and support for me and teenagers from every staff member and leader in our congregation. There is also a team mentality when it comes to pastoring and caring for teenagers and their families. As we move further away from silo-type youth ministry paradigms, this is absolutely necessary. High schoolers who operate the camera or help with media production for "big church" are connecting with adults and leaders outside the normal parameters of youth ministry. My job, then, is not to get those areas under my specific control or leadership, but instead to equip the leaders who are already there to relate to and disciple teenagers in the best way possible.

It's probable our youth ministry at Newsong is similar in some ways to that in other churches. There are calendar and programmatic elements of youth ministry we do now like we did before. I'm grateful there were already leaders, programs, and customized experiences in our church that carried the vision for intergenerational ministry before I got there. What is different is this vision no longer predominantly rests on me as a wannabe-superstar youth worker. The whole point of having a Student Integration Pastor is to debunk the notion that a paid youth ministry professional and volunteer team are the primary people who can care for and walk with teenagers in their faith journeys and only through innovative youth ministry programming. It really is possible to bring the entire church into the mission to love and disciple middle schoolers and high schoolers. It doesn't happen right away, but the vision and the journey to get there are well worth it.

Mike Park, Student Integration Pastor
June 2013

Practical Next Steps & Fuller Youth Institute

If you know me, then you know I'm all about asking, "What's next?" And if you're at all like me, then you're reading these last pages, itching to know what you need to do now. My first recommendation is to take the time to work through the questions at the end of each chapter and study the process outlined in this book. It can be a guide as you maneuver through the reimagining and redefining that needs to happen in your context. If you engage the entire process, it will pull you out of your own insanity and lead you down a sane path.

As I mentioned throughout this book, Fuller Youth Institute is really the leading voice on helping teenagers' faith stick beyond high school and into adulthood. (http://fulleryouthinstitute.org/) Their research is turning into resources that are really helping churches and organizations who want to see this tide turn. (Check out their Sticky Faith website and resources at http://stickyfaith.org/.) The Sticky Faith Launch Kit and yearlong cohort are solid starting places for lasting, practical change.

Our church participated in the Sticky Faith Cohort in 2010, and it was truly transformational. Another youth ministry leader who participated in our cohort said, "We have not gone to something else that has compared. It was the experience of an extended personalized conference that was created to intentionally help only our church and our specific needs and issues." I emphatically believe in the work FYI is doing, and I know they will be helpful in your journey as you seek to redefine what's not working and allow faith to stick in the lives of your teenagers.

May the God of all peace and truth and life guide you into reimagining and redefining your youth ministry for the sake of the kingdom and generations of adolescents to come.

"Now all glory to God, who is able, through his mighty power at work within us, to accomplish infinitely more than we might ask or think. Glory to him in the church and in Christ Jesus through all generations forever and ever! Amen" (Ephesians 3:20-21, NLT). Amen and amen.

References

Clydesdale, Tim. 2007. *The First Year Out: Understanding American Teens after High School.* Chicago, IL: University of Chicago Press.

Collins, Jim. 2001. *Good to Great.* New York: Harper-Collins Publishers Inc.

DeVries, Mark. 2008. *Sustainable Youth Ministry: Why Most Youth Ministry Doesn't Last and What Your Church Can Do About It.* Downers Grove, IL: InterVarsity Press.

Hybels, Bill. 2008. *Axiom: Powerful Leadership Proverbs.* Grand Rapids, Michigan: Zondervan.

Kotter, John. 1995. "Leading Change: Why Transformation Efforts Fail." *Harvard Business Review* (March-April), http://depts.washington.edu/ccph/pdf_files/Kotter.pdf.

Ortberg, John. 1997. *The Life You've Always Wanted: Spiritual Disciplines for Ordinary People.* Grand Rapids, Michigan: Zondervan.

Powell, Kara and Brad Griffin. 2011. *Sticky Faith, Youth Worker Edition: Practical Ideas to Nurture Long-Term Faith in Teenagers.* Grand Rapids, Michigan: Zondervan/Youth Specialties.

Rendle, Gilbert R. 1998. *Leading Change in the Congregation.* Herndon, VA: The Alban Institute, Inc.

For Further Reading

Anthony, Michelle. *Spiritual Parenting: An Awakening for Today's Families*. Colorado Springs, CO: David C. Cook, 2010.

Clark, Chap. *Hurt: Inside the World of Today's Teenagers*. Grand Rapids, Michigan: Baker Academic, 2004.

Dean, Kenda Creasy. *Almost Christian: What the Faith of Our Teenagers Is Telling the American Church*. New York: Oxford University Press, 2010.

Hybels, Bill. *Courageous Leadership: Field-Tested Strategy for the 360° Leader*. Grand Rapids, Michigan: Zondervan, 2002.

Jethani, Skye. *With: Reimagining the Way You Relate to God*. Nashville, TN: Thomas Nelson, 2011.

Joiner, Reggie. *Think Orange: Imagine the Impact When Church and Family Collide....* Colorado Springs, CO: David C. Cook, 2009.

Patterson, Kerry, Joseph Grenny, Ron McMillan, and Al Switzler. *Crucial Conversations: Tools for Talking*

When Stakes Are High, Second Edition. New York: McGraw-Hill, 2011.

Smith, Christian. *Soul Searching: The Religious and Spiritual Lives of American Teenagers*. New York: Oxford University Press, 2005.

Smith, Christian. *Souls in Transition: The Religious and Spiritual Lives of Emerging Adults*. New York: Oxford University Press, 2009.

Stevens, Jeanne. *Soul School: Enrolling in a Soulful Lifestyle for Youth Ministry*. Grand Rapids, Michigan: Zondervan/Youth Specialties, 2007.

Yaconelli, Mark. *Contemplative Youth Ministry: Practicing the Presence of Jesus*. Grand Rapids, Michigan: Zondervan/Youth Specialties, 2006.